TAROT CARD

COLORING AND LEARNING WORKBOOK

MASTERING TAROT CARD MEANINGS & SYMBOLS

CONTENTS

INTRODUCTION

Thank you for purchasing this Tarot Card coloring and learning workbook.

Learning tarot cards can often be stressful and even overwhelming.

We created this workbook as a way for you to easily learn about each tarot card by reading, looking and coloring.

Coloring has been proven to relief stress. Even if you are already highly skilled with tarot card readings, this workbook is a lot of fun to use.

As you may have noticed this workbook is 8 ½ x 11 in size to give you the maximum opportunity to really drill down and look at each tiny detail in each of the cards.

You will be moving through this coloring workbook at your own pace. Feel free to place notes on the side margins or under the description – this is your workbook – it is unique to you.

You'll be reading about each card and then coloring each card image. When you color, you'll really notice details such as details in wands or details in a major arcana card. Your brain will become familiar with each card and the tiny details you may not have noticed before. Your memory of each card may be stronger than it was before as you fully immersed yourself in the details of each card as you colored.

TAROT CARD MEANINGS
QUICK OVERVIEW

Tarot cards can be fun to use and also a great tool for divination. The challenge many people have is trying to memorize and learn each and every card.

There is an amazing amount of intricate detail in each and every card. When you are looking at an average size deck, those details may not be as noticeable.

As there are 78 cards in a classic tarot deck, learning each one can quickly become overwhelming.

To make this learning process fun, we are going to learn the basics of what each card represents and then take a very close look at each and every card by coloring them.

Once you have colored your way your way through each card, ideally the meanings clearer and the cards will spring to life. Plus, you'll have a great reference book with your own hand-colored cards inside.

Following you will find a short description of each card and then a page that contains each card for coloring. Take your time and enjoy the tarot journey.

You'll begin with the 22 Major Arcana and then progress to the 56 Minor Arcana cards.

The Major Arcana (big secret) consists of 22 cards.

The Minor Arcana (little secret) consists of 56 cards.

The Minor Arcana consists of four sets of 14 cards that represent the four elements.

Let's take a quick look at various symbols you'll encounter as you color and their meanings. Definitely go back to this list as needed when you are coloring and afterwards.

SYMBOLS AND THEIR MEANINGS IN THE TAROT DECK

As you begin coloring, you may be astounded by all the details you now see in each tarot card. By becoming familiar with the symbols and their meanings, it will become easier for you to read your tarot cards quickly and easily.

The symbols on the list below appear on the Rider Waite Tarot cards, but the list can also be used for other Tarot card decks.

Beard: wisdom
Bergen (a city in Norway) : overview
Leaves on the bars: a new beginning
Flower wreath: fertility with regard to the theme
Bunches of grapes: fertility with regard to the theme
Angels: helpers, mediators
Large coats / wide scarves: built up a lot of inner knowledge
Harness: protection
Dog: instinct
Dog with the Fool: companion
Dog by the moon: fear
Crown: connected with the higher
Laurel wreaths: laurels, honoring
Leo: power
Lemniscate (a figure eight type design): eternally continuous life force
Moon: subconscious
Horses: processes
Someone on a horse: movement
Cat: magic, being able to make/do something
Red roses: willpower, life
Snail: patience
Snake: circle of infinity
Staff in hand: wisdom
Star: connecting, radiating cosmic energy
Pisces: emotion, healing, anointing, water
Butterflies: transformation

Birds: communication with higher consciousness
Fruits: fertility related to the theme
White dress: spiritual purity
White lilies: spiritual purity
Clouds: another dimension
Sun: awareness
Sunflowers: awareness
Pillars/temple: wisdom, respect

MEANING OF WANDS, SWORDS, CUPS AND PENTACLES

Wands (element of fire): willpower
    Swords (element air): the rational mind of man, judgment, conflict(s)
    Cups (element of water): feeling, subconscious, creative ability
    Pentacles (element earth): practical, our ability to become aware of the things around us

MEANING OF THE ACE, THE PAGE, THE KNIGHT, THE KING, AND THE QUEEN

Within each set of 14 cards you will find -

An Ace (card one) - this card symbolizes the beginning of something, a wish, something that is potentially present

The cards 2 to 10:

A Page - this card represents the beginner level, the student

A Knight – this card indicates that a few things have been learned and there is the assignment to take this somewhere

A Queen - this card symbolizes the feminine perspective, the intuitive, is full of expectations

A King - this card represents the male perspective, the responsibility to the outside, the arranging and the rational aspect

THE MINOR ARCANA SYMBOLS

The 56 cards that comprise the Minor Arcana of the tarot card deck are split into suits in the same way that conventional decks of 52 playing cards are.

The minor arcana suits are pentacles, wands, cups, and swords.

The meanings of each suit are based on the four traditional elements of Earth, Air, Fire, and Water.

SYMBOLISM OF THE PENTACLE CARDS

Pentacles represent the traditional element of Earth.

This is a physical element that is grounded.

When a pentacles card occurs in a tarot spread, it either gives knowledge about the querent's physical state or discusses information about the physical (material) world in which the querent lives.

The following are some of the topics that a pentacles card may address.

Finances
Health
Property
Business or trade
Career

SYMBOLS RELATED TO CUPS

Cups represent the water element. Cups hold water, which is an easy way to remember this. Because water is an emotional element, when the cup comes in your tarot spread, it addresses themes that are mostly emotional in nature. The following are some examples of topics that a cup card could represent.

Emotions and feelings
Relationships and love
Relationships with others
Interactions with others
Attempts at creativity

Wands represent the element of fire. Imagine sparks shooting from the end of a wand to help you remember this. Fire is a primitive and powerful force associated with spirituality and higher thought. It is also connected with passion and drive.

When wands appear in a reading, they may indicate one or more of the following.

Ambitions and objectives

Purpose

Motivation and significance

Change is motivated by passion.

SYMBOLS RELATED TO SWORDS CARDS

Swords represent the air element. Imagine a sword swishing in the air to help you remember this. Air represents your mental self and the domain of thought. The following are some of the things swords may represent when they appear in a tarot reading.

Challenges
Confrontation
Courage
Disagreements and disagreements
Decisions

NUMBER SYMBOLISM IN THE TAROT

Like a standard deck of cards, each minor arcana tarot card is either a number card (aces through ten) or a court card (Page, Knight, Queen, King). Each of these has its own symbolic significance.

MINOR ARCANA COURT CARD SYMBOLISM

The court cards are the face cards of each tarot suit. Each suit contains four cards that represent the following.

Page
Youthful vitality, service

Knight
Taking action, maturing energy, and forging ahead
Queen
Empathy and compassion reign supreme.
King
Leadership, achievement, and success

WHAT THE COLORS MEAN ON TAROT CARDS

Tarot cards are bright, and the colors used in the illustrations have symbolic meanings based on the psychological effects of colors and the spiritual energy color relationship with chakras or auras. When interpreting a tarot card, consider the colors used by the artist or printer and the imagery and numerology.

Rider Waite Cards Symbolism – Color Meanings
Black – Protection, grounding, darkness or a lack of elements, disease, negativity, root chakra
Red – Grounding, safety, security, passion, rage, and the root chakra
Pink – Love, femininity, compassion, forgiveness, and the heart chakra
Orange- Sacral chakra, joy, creative ideas, optimism
Brow – Sacral chakra is associated with stability, neutrality, comfort, earthiness, muddiness, or a lack of boundaries.

Yellow – Opportunity, spontaneity, and zeal are all associated with the solar plexus chakra.
Gold – Majesty, divinity, spiritual leadership, crown chakra, or higher
Green – Healing, love, harmony, balance, enviously, bitterness, and the heart chakra
Blue – Communication, peace, self-expression, trust, melancholy, judgment, and criticism are important. The throat chakra

Purple – Third eye chakra, intuition, psychic ability, spirituality, reason, critical thinking
White – The connection to the Divine, the higher self, newness, inexperience, birth, The crown chakra
Silver – Crown chakra, emotion, sensitivity, empathy

SYMBOLS & IMAGES RELATED TO TAROT ART

Each card in most tarot decks has elaborate artwork. The symbols in the card assist the reader in interpreting the insights gained during the reading. Many of these symbols are not as they look. Keep in mind they are symbols with meaning. Here are some to watch for as you work your way through each card.

Angels:
Inspiration
Pay attention to your inner voice.
Pay close attention to the details.
Blindfold:
The client's vision is blurry.
Someone is unwilling to accept the truth.
Someone is concealing the truth.
Cat:
Unseen power
Psychic power
Before acting, be aware of all circumstances.
Dog:
Truthfulness Loyalty Honesty
We're on the right track.
Flag:
A significant shift is on the way.
Grapes:
Abundance of Fertility
Hammer:
Finishing a task
Vocation
Use force to complete a task.
Ice:
Isolation Separation
Growth as a result of a season of completion
Keys:

Opportunity for Knowledge Discovery
Lizard:
Vision
Conscious effort produces significant results.
Moon:
The passage of time
Change in Femininity
Reflection
Ocean:
Possibility
Relax and allow the universe's power to work in your life.
Emotions/emotional states
Movement
Pillar:
Balance
Look for a balanced solution.
Support
Rain:
Possibilities for Growth after Sadness
Cleansing
Ship:
Transformational personal journey
Keeping afloat
Tree:
Strength of Shelter
Regeneration
Wreath:
Spirituality, success, healing, power, psychic powers, lust, protection, and love

SYMBOLISM IN THE MAJOR ARCANA OF THE TAROT

The Rider-Waite-Smith tarot deck has 22 major arcana cards.

Each of the major arcana cards has numerology and archetype-based symbolism. The major arcana cards are numbered 0 to XXI (21) and reflect the soul's journey from innocence to enlightenment.

SYMBOLISM OF THE MAJOR ARCANA TAROT CARDS

0 The Fool – Innocence, the beginning of a journey
I The Magician – Creation, alchemy
II The High Priestess – Subconscious, intuition
III The Empress – Femininity, compassion, wise woman
IV The Emperor – Power, authority
V The Hierophant – Spiritual guidance
VI The Lovers – Relationships, partnerships
VII The Chariot – Goals, ambitions, and motivation
VIII Strength – Courage, perseverance, and standing up to life's challenges
IX The Hermit – Going within to find wisdom
X Wheel of Fortune – Impermanence, change
XI Justice – Fairness, balance
XII The Hanged Man – Patience, perspective
XIII Death – Change, new beginnings, endings
XIV Temperance – Moderation
XV The Devil – Temptation, control or lack thereof
XVI The Tower – Cataclysmic change
XVII The Star – Healing, hope, encouragement
XVIII The Moon – Subconsciousness, deep fears or emotions, reflection
XIX The Sun – Happiness, joy, excitement, awakening
XX Judgement – Recognizing how your past actions affect others, righting past misdeeds
XXI The World – Fulfillment, the end of a cycle or quest

THE MAJOR ARCANA

The classic tarot deck is split up into major arcana cards and minor arcana cards.

The Major Arcana cards are often thought of as the cream of the crop when drawing cards and as the most powerful cards.

In the Major Arcana you'll find cards including The Fool, The Star, The Magician, and The Tower.

There are 22 cards in the Major Arcana, with a variety of different interpretations.

Also - Tarot cards do not have genders. You are looking at the energy – male and female.

Everyone has both a feminine and masculine energy.

THE FOOL

The Fool, which is Number 0 is the first card in the major arcana. Contrary to what many think when this card is drawn it doesn't represent being foolish. This card represents the start of something new.

This card can represent someone who has a childlike demeanor and is more innocent. Someone who is more spontaneous, the same as a child.

In reverse, the card may be warning of being a bit too reckless or not thinking through on something – a bull in the china shop attitude.

Learning Question – What symbols have I found as I've colored this card? Write the meaning next to each symbol.

____

____

____

____

____

____

____

____

____

____

____

____

____

O
THE FOOL.

THE MAGICIAN

As you see, by the number at the top of the card, this is the number one card in the major arcana. This card is also known as THE card for manifestation. If this card is in your spread, you or the person you are doing a reading for may be working on manifesting something such as their dream life or a new job. This card can also be about creating something or the desire to do something.

If you are looking at this card in reverse, it may mean looking at something through rose colored glasses or not seeing something clearly as it really is – versus manifesting something desirable.

Learning Question – What symbols have I found as I've colored this card? Write the meaning next to each symbol.

I
THE MAGICIAN.

THE HIGH PRIESTESS

This card represents feminine energy, spirituality, intuition and nature. Remember that this card is about the divine feminine energy not the gender of being female.

The High Priestess is a card of feminine energy, nature, spirituality, and intuition. Keep in mind this is about divine feminine energy, not the gender. As was mentioned earlier in this book, Tarot does not have genders, it is simply about the energy. Everyone has both a feminine and masculine energy.

If you get this card in the reverse, it is the opposite of intuition, so maybe someone feels repressed or like they can't speak up about something.

Learning Question – What symbols have I found as I've colored this card? Write the meaning next to each symbol.

____

____

____

____

____

____

____

____

____

____

____

____

____

____

____

THE HIGH PRIESTESS

THE EMPRESS

Another divine feminine tarot card is The Empress. There are a few different interpretations, but it often means fertility (in anything, not just pregnancy), sex, motherhood, nature, and often closely connected to the high priestess.

In the reverse, consider feeling empty, alone, or being smothered as the meanings.

Learning Question – What symbols have I found as I've colored this card? Write the meaning next to each symbol.

III
THE EMPRESS.

THE EMPEROR

Now for a divine masculine card, The Emperor.

Think of this as a divine counterpart for the empress. This is someone who represents a lot of stability, hard work, leadership, and someone who follows the rules.

In terms of a love reading, the emperor tells you to be practical and logical as you approach a new partner.

In reverse, the emperor might be about being too rigid or cold.

Learning Question – What symbols have I found as I've colored this card? Write the meaning next to each symbol.

IV
THE EMPEROR.

THE HIEROPHANT

This major arcana brings forth feelings of morality and being ethical. It can be related to traditions, having good intuition, and mastering a certain area of your life. For the reverse, the hierophant might be about being more of a rebel and not following logical steps.

Learning Question – What symbols have I found as I've colored this card? Write the meaning next to each symbol.

V
THE HIEROPHANT

THE LOVERS

The important thing to remember about the lovers' card is that while it can mean a union, depending on other cards it appears with in the spread, it might also be a reminder to consider any challenges in a potential new relationship. It is about being honest and realistic, and making sure communication remains open between two people.

In the reverse, the lovers' card might mean there isn't much harmony in a particular union.

Learning Question – What symbols have I found as I've colored this card? Write the meaning next to each symbol.

VI
THE LOVERS.

THE CHARIOT

If you get the chariot card, it could be a sign of needing more control or gaining willpower in a situation. It is a reminder that you can achieve anything you want as long as you work hard toward action. In the reverse, chariot can mean the opposite, where you have no plan or direction.

Learning Question – What symbols have I found as I've colored this card? Write the meaning next to each symbol.

THE CHARIOT.

STRENGTH

The strength card is about your inner passions and strength, and really focusing on your own inner balance. Many strength cards show someone with a lion or a similar image on the card, showing that you can achieve anything you put your mind to. In the reverse, the strength card might mean feeling weak or insecure.

Learning Question – What symbols have I found as I've colored this card? Write the meaning next to each symbol.

VIII
STRENGTH.

THE HERMIT

If you get the hermit card, it could be a sign of needing to look inside for the answers. It is not just about spending time alone, though that can be part of it. But it is more about self-reflection and contemplation. In reverse, the hermit card might be the negative side of this, such as feeling lonely or isolated.

Learning Question – What symbols have I found as I've colored this card? Write the meaning next to each symbol.

THE HERMIT.

WHEEL OF FORTUNE

The wheel of fortune card is tarot is one of the most positive cards. It often signifies a positive change coming up, good fortune, and fate that might be inevitable. It can also be a sign of a cycle coming to an end soon. If you get this in reverse, consider a loss of control you might have or a string of bad luck.

Learning Question – What symbols have I found as I've colored this card? Write the meaning next to each symbol.

JUSTICE

With the justice card, it is exactly how it sounds- seeking justice and karmic. You might get this card if you are looking for fairness in a situation or seeking to achieve karmic balance. It can also reveal something truthful that has been hidden from you. On the reverse, the justice card may be warning you of someone being dishonesty or another form of unfairness.

Learning Question – What symbols have I found as I've colored this card? Write the meaning next to each symbol.

____

____

____

____

____

____

____

____

____

____

____

____

____

____

____

____

XI
JUSTICE .

THE HANGED MAN

With the hanged man, you are looking at a situation that just needs a little more patience. It is not a bad card, but it is one that reminds you sometimes you need to sit things out, take a look around, and wait until the time is right. In some situations, it also represents a release of some kind or a sacrifice.

If you get the hanged man in reverse, it might mean really needing to sacrifice something you aren't happy about losing.

Learning Question – What symbols have I found as I've colored this card? Write the meaning next to each symbol.

XII

THE HANGED MAN.

DEATH

Don't freak out if you get the death card – it's actually a good thing! Death in tarot is simply the end of a cycle. It could be a season of life coming to an end and a new season beginning. In love readings, it might be the end of one relationship and the start of another, or the ending of being single and finding love. In the reverse, the death card could represent holding on to something when it needs to be let go.

Learning Question – What symbols have I found as I've colored this card? Write the meaning next to each symbol.

XIII
DEATH.

TEMPERANCE

With the temperance card, you are being told to take it easy. It might come up during a stressful situation, or when you are moving too fast and not practicing enough patience. In the reverse, temperance could be about doing something in excess.

Learning Question – What symbols have I found as I've colored this card? Write the meaning next to each symbol.

XIV
TEMPERANCE.

THE DEVIL

There are no bad tarot cards, not even the devil card. Instead, this card is about gentle warnings of being in a relationship that might not be the best for you, or possibly about your own shadow self. It could also be about someone with an addiction who needs to be careful.

In the reverse, it is often about more freedom and gaining control.

Learning Question – What symbols have I found as I've colored this card? Write the meaning next to each symbol.

THE DEVIL .

THE TOWER

People are often afraid to get the tower card because it can represent some type of big change or danger, but in many cases, it is a good change. It could be a sudden ending you didn't see coming, but one that brings about something much better for you. If you get the tower in reverse, you might see an end of suffering.

Learning Question – What symbols have I found as I've colored this card? Write the meaning next to each symbol.

____

____

____

____

____

____

____

____

____

____

____

____

____

____

____

____

XVI
THE TOWER.

THE STAR

The star card is tarot is about getting inspiration, finding your purpose in life, and leaning on your faith or spiritual awakening. If you get the star in reverse, you might feel insecure and discouraged about something.

Learning Question – What symbols have I found as I've colored this card? Write the meaning next to each symbol.

XVII

THE STAR.

THE MOON

The moon is a beautiful card full of wonder, but also one that contains mysteries and reveals hidden truths. There could be someone with an illusion who is hiding their true selves, or a situation that requires being a little more intuitive and looking for the signs. In reverse, the moon card is often interpreting some type of confusion or fear.

Learning Question – What symbols have I found as I've colored this card? Write the meaning next to each symbol.

XVII
THE MOON.

THE SUN

The sun is by far one of the best cards in the tarot deck! This is all about luck, fortune, and happiness. If you get the sun card during a love reading, it is very likely that you are going to find the person who makes your soul fill with joy. It is one of only two tarot cards that has no reverse meaning. No matter what way it shows up, the sun card is a great card.

Learning Question – What symbols have I found as I've colored this card? Write the meaning next to each symbol.

XIX
THE SUN .

JUDGEMENT

The judgement card reminds you that there are some decisions that need to be made. You might be headed toward something new after a resurrection in your life, or perhaps being more self-reflective. The reverse can be feeling a lot of doubt or like you need clarity.

Learning Question – What symbols have I found as I've colored this card? Write the meaning next to each symbol.

JUDGEMENT.

THE WORLD

And last, is the World card. Most people also see this as a card with no reversal meanings, though some do read the reversal as something being incomplete. With the world card, a cycle has ended and something new is on the horizon. This is a very good and happy card full of balance and fulfillment. It could be a manifestation that is finally coming true.

Learning Question – What symbols have I found as I've colored this card? Write the meaning next to each symbol.

XXI
THE WORLD.

MINOR ARCANA

The next set of tarot cards to learn are the minor arcana.

These are the remaining 56 cards and include different suits, similar to what you would find in playing cards.

The suits include cups, wands, pentacles, and swords. Not only does each suit mean something different, but each card within these suits also has its own interpretation. Similar to the major arcana, they can also be read differently if they show up in reverse.

CUPS

Think of cups as you are filling up a cup with water. The cups suit is all about your emotions and feelings, as well as give a lot of insight into connections. If you are familiar with astrology, you know that the water signs of the zodiac (Pisces, Scorpio, Cancer) are the most emotional of all the signs. This might be an easy way to interpret cup cards.

ACE OF CUPS

With the ace of cups, you might have new feelings about something or have been using your intuition a lot more recently. In the reverse, this tarot card could be about some type of emotional blockage or feeling empty inside.

Learning Question – What symbols have I found as I've colored this card? Write the meaning next to each symbol.

ACE of CUPS.

TWO OF CUPS

Think of the two of cups as two people coming together in union. It can be the start of a new relationship or a partnership. Remember this doesn't have to be a romantic union. In the reverse, the two of cups might be about a broken relationship or partnership or some type of imbalance in your life.

Learning Question – What symbols have I found as I've colored this card? Write the meaning next to each symbol.

II

THREE OF CUPS

The three of cups is also about union, but more about community and friendship. It is often seen as three friends on the card, depicted in a happy and joyous scene. With the reverse, consider if gossip or isolation has been in your life recently.

Learning Question – What symbols have I found as I've colored this card? Write the meaning next to each symbol.

III

FOUR OF CUPS

The four of cups is often associated with contemplating something, but often with a feeling of apathy. You might feel a little disconnected from a situation or person in your life. The reverse is about being more aware and having clarity.

Learning Question – What symbols have I found as I've colored this card? Write the meaning next to each symbol.

IV

FIVE OF CUPS

The five of cups tarot card is another slightly negative card, perhaps reminding you not to feel sorry for yourself or to focus on your grief. The reverse could mean more peace is coming in your life.

Learning Question – What symbols have I found as I've colored this card? Write the meaning next to each symbol.

V

SIX OF CUPS

The six of cups is a positive, happy cards. You might be heading to healing some wounds in your life, being more grateful for your family, and just staying in the same position with a new appreciation for it. The reverse is often about moving on or moving forward.

Learning Question – What symbols have I found as I've colored this card? Write the meaning next to each symbol.

VI

SEVEN OF CUPS

The seven of cups typically shows up when you have been trying to manifest or figure out what to do next. Maybe you are daydreaming or looking for your purpose in life. In the reverse, seven of cups might show some confusion about your next steps.

Learning Question – What symbols have I found as I've colored this card? Write the meaning next to each symbol.

VII

EIGHT OF CUPS

With the eight of cups, you are looking to walk away from a situation. It is not really avoiding someone, but just needing to leave someone behind. However, if you get this in the reverse, it could be that you are avoiding making a move or fearing this change.

Learning Question – What symbols have I found as I've colored this card? Write the meaning next to each symbol.

VIII

NINE OF CUPS

If you get the nine of cups, you might have a wish being granted soon, or are looking for the finer things in life. In the reverse, it could mean bragging or being a little smug about the things you have in your life.

Learning Question – What symbols have I found as I've colored this card? Write the meaning next to each symbol.

IX

TEN OF CUPS

Everyone wants the ten of cups! This is the ultimate wish fulfillment. Your dreams are coming true, and you are finding your manifestations happening in your life. But if you get it in the reverse, it might mean the opposite, where some of your dreams are shifting or are gone altogether.

Learning Question – What symbols have I found as I've colored this card? Write the meaning next to each symbol.

PAGE OF CUPS

The page of cups is a card of emotional maturity, having a happy surprise occur in your life, and being a dreamer. If you get it in the reverse, you might be dealing with some type of disappointment.

Learning Question – What symbols have I found as I've colored this card? Write the meaning next to each symbol.

____

____

____

____

____

____

____

____

____

____

____

____

____

____

____

____

____

PAGE of CUPS.

KNIGHT OF CUPS

The knight of cups is a very romantic card. It is great news if this shows up in your reading and you are looking for romance. It can also mean following your heart or being creative in other areas of your life. If you get it reversed, you might be dealing with a poor mood.

Learning Question – What symbols have I found as I've colored this card? Write the meaning next to each symbol.

KNIGHT *of* CUPS.

QUEEN OF CUPS

With the queen of cups, you are in a calm and comfortable environment. You likely feel very stable in yourself, secure, and compassionate. But if you get this in the reverse, be aware of co-dependency in others or feeling low self-esteem.

Learning Question – What symbols have I found as I've colored this card? Write the meaning next to each symbol.

QUEEN of CUPS.

KING OF CUPS

The kind of cups is a divine masculine energy, where you feel very controlled and balanced. You give out good advice to those who come to you and are often stable in your life. In the reverse, it could mean an energy of being irritable, unhelpful to others, and unstable.

Learning Question – What symbols have I found as I've colored this card? Write the meaning next to each symbol.

KING of CUPS.

III

WANDS

Next is the wands suit, which are nearly opposite of water. These represent fire, so they can be a lot about taking action to make decisions, and are frequently infused with feelings of high energy and passion.

ACE OF WANDS

When you get the ace of wands, it represents someone who is very passionate, bold, and creative. This is something they are born with, not that they learn. The reverse is someone with lack of creativity or passion.

Learning Question – What symbols have I found as I've colored this card? Write the meaning next to each symbol.

ACE of WANDS.

TWO OF WANDS

In tarot, the two of wands card is typically about making decisions and plans for what you want in the future. The reverse is often having a fear of the unknown and not taking action because of that fear.

Learning Question – What symbols have I found as I've colored this card? Write the meaning next to each symbol.

II

THREE OF WANDS

If you get the three of wands, the person you are reading for is likely planning for the future. It can mean growth or simply looking ahead at what comes next. The reversal might be having some kind of delays or challenges with these plans.

Learning Question – What symbols have I found as I've colored this card? Write the meaning next to each symbol.

FOUR OF WANDS

With the four of wands, it is all about celebration and happiness. There is a lot of gratitude and community with this card. In the reverse, it speaks of loneliness or conflicts with other people.

Learning Question – What symbols have I found as I've colored this card? Write the meaning next to each symbol.

IV

FIVE OF WANDS

The five of wands typically is about some type of conflict or competition with a group of people. On the tarot card, you see five people who are holding their wands in the air, speaking of perhaps some rivalry. Though in reverse, it can be read as avoiding challenges.

Learning Question – What symbols have I found as I've colored this card? Write the meaning next to each symbol.

V

SIX OF WANDS

The six of wands is a card about pride, accomplishments, victory, and success. It can often be about getting acknowledgement for your accomplishments. In the reverse, six of wands might be about lack of recognition.

Learning Question – What symbols have I found as I've colored this card? Write the meaning next to each symbol.

SEVEN OF WANDS

If you pull the seven of wands, you are standing your ground and are in control. You might be a little defensive, but are doing so in order to stay where you are and be more assertive. The reverse could represent someone giving up or not being confident.

Learning Question – What symbols have I found as I've colored this card? Write the meaning next to each symbol.

# VII

EIGHT OF WANDS

With the eight of wands, it is about keeping up momentum and continuing to move forward, perhaps at a faster pace than what you are used to. You often make rapid decisions and get going quickly. If you get it in reverse, you are waiting for too long or slowing down.

Learning Question – What symbols have I found as I've colored this card? Write the meaning next to each symbol.

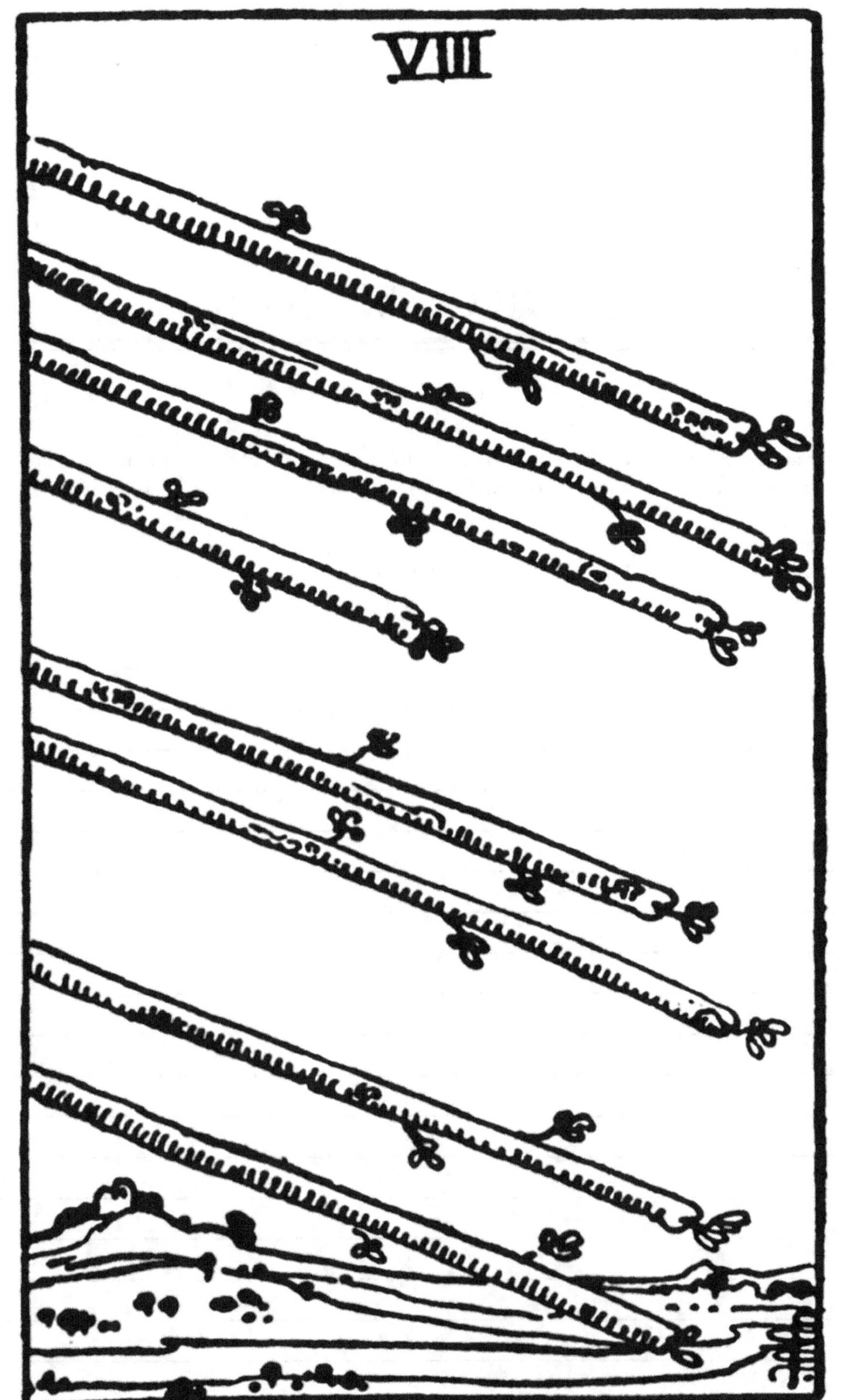

VIII

NINE OF WANDS

The nine of wands talks about resilience and grit. It is for a person or situation where there are challenges, but the person stays firm with their actions and holds onto hope. In reverse, there is a lot of fatigue and overwhelm.

Learning Question – What symbols have I found as I've colored this card? Write the meaning next to each symbol.

IX

TEN OF WANDS

With the ten of wands, you are accomplishing great things, but you might also be burdened by doing too much. It reminds you to take a step back and analyze how things are going in your life. The reverse is being even more stressed about a situation.

Learning Question – What symbols have I found as I've colored this card? Write the meaning next to each symbol.

X

PAGE OF WANDS

The page of wands is all about excitement and freedom. This is a person who acts quickly and is adventurous in love and life. In the reverse, they might get bored easily, have no direction, or be in the middle of conflict.

Learning Question – What symbols have I found as I've colored this card? Write the meaning next to each symbol.

PAGE of WANDS.

KNIGHT OF WANDS

With the knight of wands, it is representing something very straightforward, but could also be someone who is fearless in their approach. In the reverse, the knight of wands is too impulsive.

Learning Question – What symbols have I found as I've colored this card? Write the meaning next to each symbol.

KNIGHT of WANDS.

QUEEN OF WANDS

The queen of wands is very determined and courageous. This energy is that of someone who knows their life purpose and goes after it without hesitation. The reverse is an energy of pettiness and jealousy.

Learning Question – What symbols have I found as I've colored this card? Write the meaning next to each symbol.

QUEEN of WANDS.

KING OF WANDS

The king of wands in tarot is a leader and someone who uses creativity and passion to make smart choices in life. The reverse is often impulsive and sometimes overbearing.

Learning Question – What symbols have I found as I've colored this card? Write the meaning next to each symbol.

KING of WANDS

PENTACLES

The pentacle suit of cards is closely connected to the earth, so not only are they more practical, but also very closely associated with money, manifestations, and wealth.

ACE OF PENTACLES

The ace of pentacles is a very prosperous card, particularly when it comes to new businesses or opportunities. For many people, this is their "entrepreneur" tarot card. In the reverse, it could be a bad investment or an opportunity you let slip through your fingers.

Learning Question – What symbols have I found as I've colored this card? Write the meaning next to each symbol.

ACE of PENTACLES

TWO OF PENTACLES

The two of pentacles card is interpreted as adapting to change and putting things into perspective. You become more organized and start finding balance. If it lands in the reverse, it might mean a loss of that balance.

Learning Question – What symbols have I found as I've colored this card? Write the meaning next to each symbol.

THREE OF PENTACLES

With a three of pentacles, the energy is that of collaborating with other people. It could be romantic, but mostly is about teamwork. The reverse of this card is a lack of organization and conflict between partners or in a group.

Learning Question – What symbols have I found as I've colored this card? Write the meaning next to each symbol.

FOUR OF PENTACLES

If you get the four of pentacles, consider an energy of financial security through the means of saving, setting a budget, or being frugal. The reversal is either being greedy or spending without thinking it through.

Learning Question – What symbols have I found as I've colored this card? Write the meaning next to each symbol.

IV

FIVE OF PENTACLES

With the five of pentacles, it goes even further into poverty and more of a need or being insecure in finances and in life. However, the reversal can be more positive, looking at an improvement in finances.

Learning Question – What symbols have I found as I've colored this card? Write the meaning next to each symbol.

____

____

____

____

____

____

____

____

____

____

____

____

____

____

____

____

SIX OF PENTACLES

The six of pentacles tarot card offers up an energy of sharing and being more generous. You might be donating to a cause or the energy is that of sharing the wealth. The reverse is being stingy and possibly offering only with expectations of getting something back.

Learning Question – What symbols have I found as I've colored this card? Write the meaning next to each symbol.

SEVEN OF PENTACLES

As we move through the pentacles suit, we get to the seven of pentacles, where it is about hard work and persevering. This is someone who knows what they need to do and doesn't give up. The reversal can be someone who is lazy or simply gets distracted.

Learning Question – What symbols have I found as I've colored this card? Write the meaning next to each symbol.

____

____

____

____

____

____

____

Learning Question – What symbols have I found as I've colored this card? Write the meaning next to each symbol.

____

____

____

____

____

____

____

VII

EIGHT OF PENTACLES

This tarot card is about raising your standards when it comes to wealth and your passions in life. If it lands in the reverse, you might be feeling uninspired or lacking motivation to work on your goals.

Learning Question – What symbols have I found as I've colored this card? Write the meaning next to each symbol.

VIII

NINE OF PENTACLES

With the nine of pentacles, you are being rewarded for all your hard work, but the reversal might mean spending your rewards too quickly or living beyond your means.

Learning Question – What symbols have I found as I've colored this card? Write the meaning next to each symbol.

IX

TEN OF PENTACLES

Finally, there is the ten of pentacles. This card helps set you up for the future. It is the most prosperous of all pentacles card where you get surprise money or find wealth and fame. With the reversal, you have a lack of stability.

Learning Question – What symbols have I found as I've colored this card? Write the meaning next to each symbol.

X

PAGE OF PENTACLES

With the page of pentacles, there are feelings of desire and ambition. This is someone similar to a Virgo or Capricorn who go after what they want in a very efficient way. But in the reverse, this is someone who doesn't work hard and lacks commitment.

Learning Question – What symbols have I found as I've colored this card? Write the meaning next to each symbol.

PAGE of PENTACLES.

KNIGHT OF PENTACLES

The knight of pentacles is a card to represent hard work and doing what needs to be done. You are not lazy or inefficient, unless this card shows up in the reverse.

Learning Question – What symbols have I found as I've colored this card? Write the meaning next to each symbol.

PAGE of PENTACLES

QUEEN OF PENTACLES

The queen of pentacles is an energy of comfort, security in finances, and being vry stable. This is a practical energy and someone who thinks with their head. The reverse is someone who tends to get jealous easily and might smother those they love.

Learning Question – What symbols have I found as I've colored this card? Write the meaning next to each symbol.

QUEEN of PENTACLES

KING OF PENTACLES

The king of pentacles is a wonderful card for abundance. It is excellent to get if you are trying to manifest something or looking for more stability and security. If it lands in the reverse, it could be about over-indulgence and greed.

Learning Question – What symbols have I found as I've colored this card? Write the meaning next to each symbol.

KING of PENTACLES.

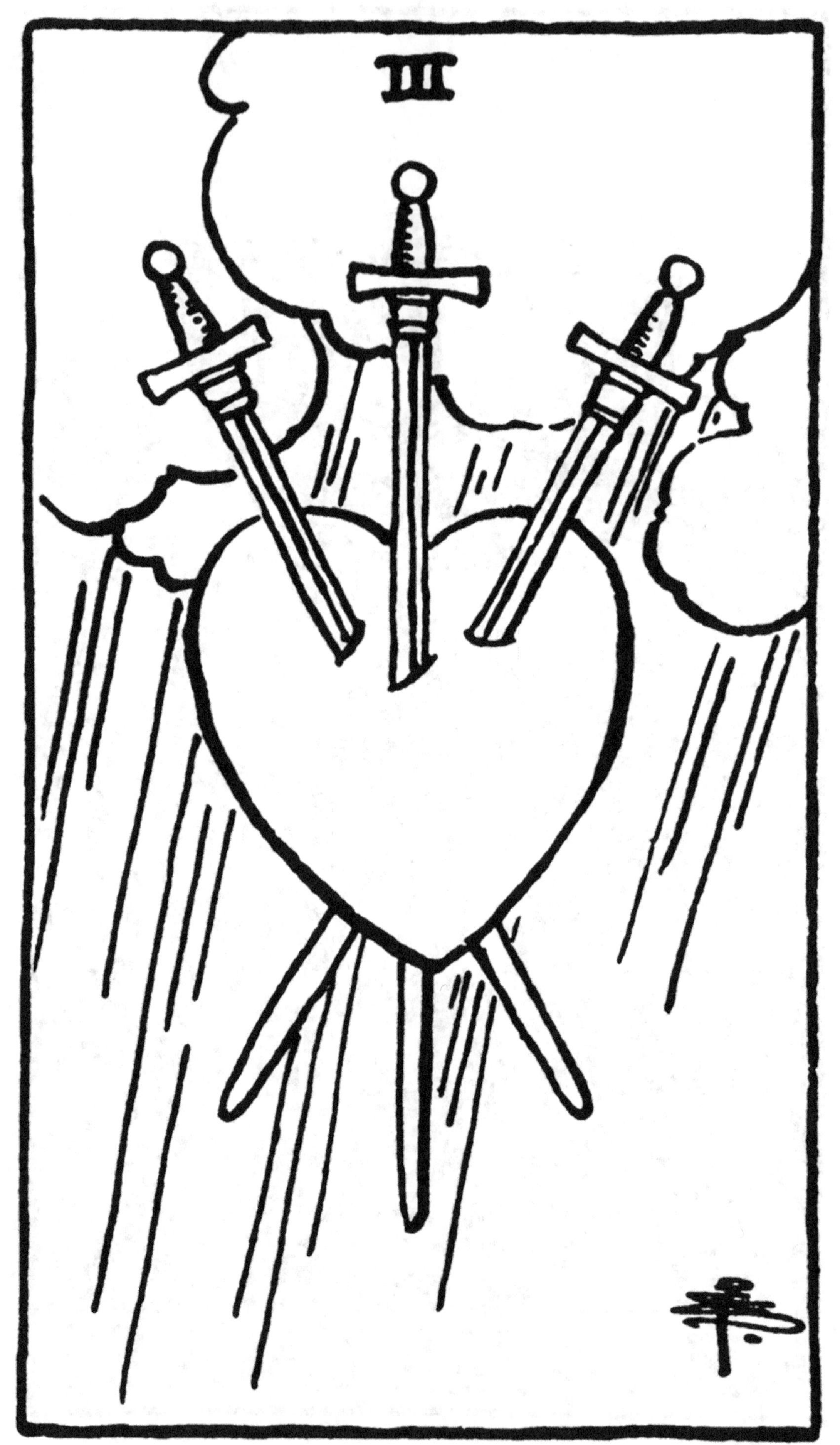

III

SWORDS

Lastly, there are the suit of swords, which are the air cards. Think of swinging a sword in the air, and it can help you remember this association. With sword cards, they are typically more about intelligence, thoughts, and making important decisions. These can also be closely related to manifesting.

ACE OF SWORDS

The ace of swords is a card of breaking through and finding clarity. This is someone who is seeing much more clearly. In reverse, there might be some chaotic energy and a lot of confusion.

Learning Question – What symbols have I found as I've colored this card? Write the meaning next to each symbol.

ACE of SWORDS.

TWO OF SWORDS

With the two of swords, the energy is about indecision and hitting a block. This energy has difficulty making a choice, either from lack of clarity or fear. The reversal of the two of swords is feeling like there is no good choice.

Learning Question – What symbols have I found as I've colored this card? Write the meaning next to each symbol.

THREE OF SWORDS

In tarot, the three of swords card is one of grief, sadness, or heartbreak. For a love reading, it could mean a couple that is breaking up. In a life reading, there might be another situation causing emotional turmoil for this person. The reversal is one of acceptance and forgiveness.

Learning Question – What symbols have I found as I've colored this card? Write the meaning next to each symbol.

III

FOUR OF SWORDS

The four of swords is about contemplating and getting rest. You might come from a period of working hard and trying to take action, but now you are being asked to step back and reassess. If it is in the reverse, you are facing burnout or under a lot of stress.

Learning Question – What symbols have I found as I've colored this card? Write the meaning next to each symbol.

FIVE OF SWORDS

The five of swords card is an energy of being sneaky and cheating, lying, or stealing to get a win. The reversal can either be forgiveness or trying to reconcile.

Learning Question – What symbols have I found as I've colored this card? Write the meaning next to each symbol.

____

____

____

____

____

____

____

____

____

____

____

____

____

____

____

____

____

____

SIX OF SWORDS

Six of swords is a card of transition and moving on. It is frequently associated with moving on from a person or relationship, but can be anything in life that feels like a new start. The reversal is about resisting this change or having emotional baggage.

Learning Question – What symbols have I found as I've colored this card? Write the meaning next to each symbol.

VI

SEVEN OF SWORDS

With the seven of swords, there is a lot of deception and hidden agendas. The person you are dealing with is likely hiding something, especially if this comes up with the Moon card. The reversal is often someone who no longer wants to deceives and is going to be honest.

Learning Question – What symbols have I found as I've colored this card? Write the meaning next to each symbol.

VIII

NINE OF SWORDS

The nine of swords card has a lot of anxiety and feelings of abandonment or trauma. But if it shows up in the reverse, this person is looking for help.

Learning Question – What symbols have I found as I've colored this card? Write the meaning next to each symbol.

IX

TEN OF SWORDS

Ten of swords in tarot is one of a feeling of failure and defeat. It might be in a relationship, work, or personal situation. The reversal is seeing it from a new perspective where the only way to go from here is up.

Learning Question – What symbols have I found as I've colored this card? Write the meaning next to each symbol.

X

PAGE OF SWORDS

In tarot, the page of swords card is one that reveals being a little restless, curious, and looking for more insight. In the reverse, it could mean someone who is being manipulative or not following up their words with actions.

Learning Question – What symbols have I found as I've colored this card? Write the meaning next to each symbol.

PAGE of SWORDS.

KNIGHT OF SWORDS

With the knight of swords, you are looking at an energy of being impulsive and acting swiftly to defend what you believe in. The reverse is an energy of no direction and not taking responsibility.

Learning Question – What symbols have I found as I've colored this card? Write the meaning next to each symbol.

KNIGHT of SWORDS .

QUEEN OF SWORDS

The queen of swords is a very complex person who is highly intuitive and has a clear mind, but in the reverse, she is bitter and sometimes resentful.

Learning Question – What symbols have I found as I've colored this card? Write the meaning next to each symbol.

QUEEN of SWORDS.

KING OF SWORDS

The king of swords is a tarot card about truth and discipline. This is someone who makes decisions based on their mind, not their heart. In the reverse, the king of swords might be weak or even cruel.

Learning Question – What symbols have I found as I've colored this card? Write the meaning next to each symbol.

KING of SWORDS.